WORLD WAR II

The Full Story

North Africa and Europe

1940–1945

Published by Brown Bear Books Ltd
4877 N. Circulo Bujia
Tucson, AZ 85718
USA

and

First Floor
9-17 St. Albans Place
London N1 0NX

ISBN: 978-1-78121-230-1

Library of Congress Cataloging-in-Publication
Data available upon request

Managing Editor: Tim Cooke
Designer: Lynne Lennon
Picture Researcher: Andrew Webb
Picture Manager: Sophie Mortimer
Editorial Director: Lindsey Lowe
Design Manager: Keith Davis
Children's Publisher: Anne O'Daly
Production Director: Alastair Gourlay

Manufactured in the United States of America

CPSIA compliance information: Batch# AG/5566

CONTENTS

Introduction 4

CHAPTER 1
Britain Stands Alone 6

CHAPTER 2
North Africa 10

CHAPTER 3
Sicily and Italy 16

CHAPTER 4
The Eastern Front....................................22

CHAPTER 5
The Invasion of Europe............................30

CHAPTER 6
The Fall of Germany................................38

Timeline of World War II....................44
Glossary 46
Further Resources................................47
Index..48

INTRODUCTION

When France surrendered to the Germans in June 1940, Adolf Hitler occupied most of northwestern Europe. The British Army had been forced to retreat from the beaches of the Belgian port of Dunkirk. The fall of France to the Germans had effects farther afield. The French colonies in North Africa—Algeria, Tunisia, and Morocco—came under the control of the puppet French government the Germans put in place at Vichy. The Germans' Italian allies, meanwhile, governed Libya, and used it as a base for attacking the British forces in Egypt.

Resisting Hitler

Hitler planned Operation Sealion, the invasion of Britain across the English Channel. But Britain did not stand entirely alone. U.S. president Franklin D. Roosevelt introduced the Lend-Lease Act in March 1941. The act allowed the United States to provide the Allied nations with war supplies on the understanding that America would be paid back later. Merchant ships carried supplies across the Atlantic Ocean. German U-boats (submarines) caused heavy losses until the Allies introduced a system in which ships traveled in convoys guarded by warships.

➔ U.S. soldiers move inland from Omaha Beach after the Allied landings on D-Day, June 6, 1944.

→ U.S. troops march through Carentan after the Allied invasion of France on D-Day, June 6, 1945.

The United States Enters the War

On December 7, 1941, Japanese aircraft attacked the U.S. Pacific Fleet at Pearl Harbor in Hawaii. Next day, the United States declared war on Japan. Three days later, Japan's allies Germany and Italy declared war on the United States.

U.S. involvement changed the war dramatically. American and British officers had held secret talks early in 1941 about military cooperation. After Pearl Harbor, the British Prime Minister Winston Churchill visited Roosevelt in Washington, D.C. At a conference codenamed Arcadia, they agreed that the Allies would prioritize the defeat of Germany over that of Japan. The first significant fighting was likely to be in North Africa.

BRITAIN STANDS ALONE

By summer 1940, things looked bleak for Britain. Its land forces had been crushed. Now Germany threatened to invade.

British fighter pilots rush to their Hurricane planes in 1940.

Hitler ordered his army to prepare for the invasion of Britain. Despite its retreat from France in June, however, Britain still had a powerful navy and air force that had to be defeated before any invasion could begin.

The German air force (the Luftwaffe) planned to defeat the Royal Air Force (RAF) Fighter Command. At the beginning of June 1940, the RAF had only 331 fighter planes. However, British factories were soon producing 500 Spitfire and Hurricane planes a month. The RAF also had a new network of radar stations along the English coast that could detect approaching enemy aircraft. The stations alerted RAF squadrons to "scramble," or rush to get their planes airborne.

The Battle of Britain

The Battle of Britain began in July 1940, when the Luftwaffe attacked British ships in the English Channel. In the face of continuing British resistance, Hitler ordered the Luftwaffe to focus on the destruction of the RAF. The German campaign to defeat Britain began on

August 15, with a series of daily attacks by the Luftwaffe on British airfields. The skies above southern Britain were filled with vapor trails as fighters tried to outmaneuver one another in dogfights.

The stress of daily combat deeply affected both British and German pilots. Between August 24 and September 7, however, the Luftwaffe lost 380 aircraft, and despite some German successes, Britain managed to keep 600 aircraft operational each day. Both sides were suffering from the intense aerial combat, but neither was giving way.

⬇ Firefighters tackle a blaze in London after a Luftwaffe air raid.

KEY THEMES

AIR RAIDS

During the Blitz of 1940 and 1941, Londoners became used to nightly bombing raids. A "blackout" was introduced to try to confuse the bombers. All sources of light had to be hidden. Car headlights were reduced to a thin strip by using black tape. As soon as enemy aircraft were detected, sirens sounded to warn civilians. People took cover for the night in cellars, subway stations, or purpose-built air-raid shelters.

→ This famous photograph shows St Paul's Cathedral in London emerging like a beacon from smoke caused by bombing.

Bombing Begins

On August 24, 1941, a flight of German bombers accidentally dropped their bombs over London. City bombing had so far been avoided by both sides through fear of escalating the war against civilians. After the London attack, Churchill authorized a raid on Berlin by 81 bombers the following night. Hitler was enraged. With fall approaching fast, and the opportunity to launch Operation Sealion, the invasion of Britain, slipping from his grasp, he ordered that the Luftwaffe switch its focus from the airfields to bombing London and Britain's other major cities.

The Germans believed that the British would have to use every available fighter to protect their cities, and that this would leave the airfields unprotected, leading to the RAF's destruction. This did not happen, however. By taking the pressure off the airfields, the Luftwaffe allowed the RAF a breathing space to reorganize.

The Blitz

The German bombing campaign against London began on September 7, when 2,000 Londoners were either killed or injured, and the London docks were set on fire. The bombers returned every night for 57 nights, leaving nearly 20,000 Londoners dead and destroying a million homes. From mid-November other cities also suffered. The worst hit included industrial centers such as Coventry, Sheffield, and Birmingham, and ports such as Portsmouth and Swansea. Only in May 1941 did the Blitz slacken in pace. The Germans began to pull aircraft east ready for the planned invasion of the Soviet Union. The Blitz had failed to crush Britain or destroy the morale of its people and its failure had forced Hitler to suspend Operation Sealion. The focus of the Allies now shifted to North Africa.

⬇ Bystanders inspect a bomb crater in front of the Bank of England.

EYEWITNESS ACCOUNT

"One night there was only one woman on the platform. The sirens went and the lady said to me, 'We have to go down to the luggage subway.' So we went underground to a dark passage. Suddenly she grabbed me and shouted, 'A rat! A rat!' I'd rather have an air raid than a rat. So we went back on the platform."

Ivy Oates
Student,
Birmingham, 1940

NORTH AFRICA

With Germany in control of mainland Europe, in late 1940 the focus of fighting moved to North Africa, where Italy, France, and Britain were all colonial powers.

The Italian dictator Benito Mussolini wanted to defeat British forces in Africa. He wanted to add to Italy's colonies in Libya in the north, and Ethiopia, Eritrea, and Somaliland in the east. The 200,000 Italians in Libya faced 63,500 British troops in Egypt and Palestine who were there to defend the Suez Canal and the British oilfields of the Middle East.

Italian Victories

In September 1940 the Italians advanced from Libya to Sidi Barrani, 60 miles (95 km) inside British Egypt. The British counterattacked in December, advancing rapidly into Libya and capturing 80,000 Italian prisoners before they halted. They were so far ahead of their bases it was difficult to keep them supplied.

→ British troops fire a 25-pounder gun as they defend a position against the Italians.

← Sherman tanks of Britain's Eighth Army advance through the desert.

MEDITERRANEAN CAMPAIGN

The fighting in North Africa was linked to a wider campaign for control of the Mediterranean Sea. The Germans and Italians seized Greece in April 1941 and Crete a month later. They failed to bomb the key strategic island of Malta into submission, however, but took a heavy toll of convoys heading to and from the island. At the end of 1941, the battle over Mediterranean supply lines continued.

Italian Defeat in East Africa

Italian raids into British territory in East Africa were overturned by November 1941, but in North Africa the British faced German troops. In February 1941, the new Afrika Korps arrived in Libya led by Major General Erwin Rommel. Rommel launched a major offensive east, halting on April 27 at the Egyptian border. His advance had been brilliant, but costly in terms of casualties and tanks. By October,

ERWIN ROMMEL

Remembered best for his victories in Africa, Erwin Rommel was an expert tactician. He brilliantly led a tank division during the invasion of France before taking charge of the Afrika Korps. In June 1942 he became Germany's youngest ever field marshal after capturing Tobruk. In June 1944, he was found to be involved in a plot to kill Hitler. He was later forced to kill himself to protect his family.

the advance was bogged down by a lack of fuel for tanks and other vehicles. Rommel retreated back into Libya, but by early February 1942 had advanced again more than 400 miles (644 km) east. The British retreated to the fortified Gazala Line, but Rommel broke through in the desert, forcing the Eighth Army to withdraw into Egypt, leaving the Allied-held port of Tobruk in Libya isolated.

Battles of El Alamein

The Eighth Army fell back to a defensive line south of the Egyptian coastal village of El Alamein. A defensive line based on the village became the scene of three major battles. In the first, which began on July 1, 1942, Rommel's panzer divisions were halted by Allied counterattacks.

Meanwhile Churchill was worried about the Allied failure to match the Germans in armored warfare. He also made

↓ Watched by British soldiers, U.S. troops bring a gun ashore in November 1942.

➔ An Afrika Korps machine gun crew lies in wait. The guns could fire 900 rounds per minute.

General Bernard Montgomery commander of the Eighth Army, hoping that he would bring more aggression to the campaign. Instead, it was Rommel who launched a second offensive on August 30. Shortages of fuel and ammunition brought what was called the Battle of Alam El Halfa to a close.

Montgomery launched his own attack on October 23. This Second Battle of El Alamein was a turning point for the Allies not only in North Africa but also in the wider war. Montgomery used his superior supply lines to launch a huge artillery bombardment. When the advance faltered, he sent in reinforcements. The Afrika Korps were exhausted and near defeat. They had lost 7,000 men and had fewer than 50 tanks. The Allies had 600

OPERATION TORCH

U.S. troops entered the war in Operation Torch, three Allied landings in Morocco and Algeria, on November 8, 1942. The Allies faced varying degrees of resistance from Vichy French forces. The French forces in Morocco sided with the Allies. They advanced along the coast into Tunisia, where Rommel was trapped between the Allied First Army in the west and the British Eighth Army in the east.

tanks and total air superiority. On November 2, Rommel ordered a retreat despite receiving orders from Hitler to stand firm. It was the first major defeat of the war for the Germans.

The Battle for Tunisia

By January 23, 1943, Rommel had retreated more than 1,000 miles (1,600 km) from El Alamein to Mareth in Tunisia. Meanwhile U.S., British, and French forces pushed east along the North African coast from Morocco and Algeria. On November 25, 1942, this Allied First

↓ British troops come under fire during the First Battle of El Alamein in July 1942.

→ Tunisians in Tunis,
the capital city,
celebrate the Allied
victory in May 1943.

Army had begun an offensive to seize Tunisia. They were halted by Rommel's strong defensive line but Montgomery's Eighth Army continued to bear down on the Afrika Korps from the southeast.

In February 1943, Rommel struck west at the U.S. forces. On February 18, German forces captured the Kasserine Pass, inflicting heavy losses. The British halted the advance. Rommel withdrew and struck east against the Eighth Army, but lost more than a third of his 150 tanks to British mines and antitank guns.

Two weeks later, on March 20, British and New Zealand troops attacked the Mareth Line. After five days fighting, the New Zealanders broke through and threatened to encircle the Germans. Rommel retreated. Suffering from ill health, he returned to Germany.

Retreat and Surrender

Axis troops retreated into northeastern Tunisia, where the German high command ordered them to fight on. By April 1943, Axis defenses were ranged along a front protecting the capital,

Tunis, and the port of Bizerte. The Allies broke through on May 6 and captured the cities. On May 13, the final 250,000 Axis troops surrendered.

The Axis had lost a million troops and thousands of tanks in North Africa. The losses, combined with those on the Soviet Front, were a serious blow to Hitler's war effort. The Allies had suffered heavy casualties, but had secured control of Africa and the southern shores of the Mediterranean. U.S. forces had gained combat experience, and the Allies were now in a position to attack Nazi-occupied Europe from the south.

SICILY AND ITALY

After the Axis surrender in North Africa in May 1943, the Allies decided to attack Nazi-occupied Europe from the south, invading Italy via the island of Sicily.

Operation Husky, as the campaign was called, would involve 160,000 Allied troops from North Africa in the largest amphibious landing yet seen. U.S. General Dwight D. Eisenhower and the British commander General Bernard Montgomery led the joint operation. To gain the advantage of surprise, the Allies staged an elaborate hoax. In Operation Mincemeat, British intelligence planted fake documents on a corpse that was dumped in the Mediterranean.

⬇ British troops wade ashore during the Allied landings in Sicily in July 1943.

← British soldiers search for hidden German defenders on Sicily in July 1943. By mid-August, 102,000 German troops had evacuated the island to the Italian mainland.

When the body washed ashore, the documents convinced the German High Command that the Allies were planning to land on Greece and Crete, rather than Sicily. In summer of 1943, Hitler ordered his troops to Greece from their positions in France and elsewhere in Europe.

Defense of Sicily

The German redeployment left just two German armored divisions on Sicily, together with 230,000 Italian troops. On the morning of July 10, 1943, the Allies launched combined amphibious and parachute landings. The Italians defending the beaches soon surrendered. The Germans offered more resistance, but with many troops still in Greece they were heavily outnumbered. Over the next five weeks U.S. armored corps from the

EYEWITNESS ACCOUNT

“The first wounded began to crawl back over the ridge. They all told the same story. They fired their bazookas at the front plate of German tanks, and then the tanks swiveled their huge 88-mm guns at them and fired at the individual infantrymen. By this time the tanks could be heard, although I could not see any because of the smoke and dust and the cover of vegetation.”

Gen. James Gavin
82nd Airborne Division,
Sicily, July 1943

Seventh Army commanded by General George S. Patton moved toward the northwest coast of Sicily and then east to the town of Messina. Montgomery's British troops moved up the east coast.

By July 23, the Allies had 467,000 troops on Sicily and their numerical superiority was beginning to show. Meanwhile, the Italian government was collapsing as an invasion of the mainland came closer. On July 25, 1943, the King of Italy ordered the arrest of the country's fascist dictator, Benito Mussolini.

Victory in Sicily

Realizing that he could no longer defend Sicily, the German commander Field Marshal Albert Kesselring ordered his men to retreat across the Strait of Messina to the mainland. By August 17, the last German troops had crossed to the mainland. The month-long battle had cost the Allies far fewer casualties than they had expected.

An Allied invasion of Italy threatened to turn the country into a battlefield. To avoid this, Italian politicians distanced themselves from the Nazis. Worried that Italy would switch sides, Hitler sent German reinforcements to Italy.

On September 3, 1943, the Italians signed an armistice with the Allies. The Germans seized key positions in Rome and central and north Italy. Only on the islands of Corsica and Sardinia did Italian forces expel the Germans.

Allied Invasion of Italy

Allied troops landed at Salerno, south of Naples in southern Italy, on September 9. The Allies met fierce resistance from Marshal Kesselring's troops as they secured a beachhead. The landings were

➔ Allied bombs explode around the monastery of Monte Cassino.

← The Italians sign the armistice with the Allies on September 3, 1943. Much of Italy was still occupied by German forces.

costly in terms of casualties, but they gave the Allies a starting point for an advance northward through Italy.

Further north, Kesselring had built defensive lines stretching from the west to east coasts of the peninsula to protect Rome. The main Gustav Line was 10 miles (16 km) deep in places, and heavily fortified with minefields, machine-gun posts, and barbed wire. To break through the Gustav Line, the Allies had to take

MONTE CASSINO

The 1,693-foot (519 m) peak of Monte Cassino blocked the Allies' way north. It was defended by German elite paratroopers and panzer troops. It took the Allies four attempts to capture the town between January 17 and May 18, 1944. During this time, the Allies deliberately bombed the ancient monastery on the mountain peak in order to stop the Germans fortifying it.

KEY EVENTS

RESCUE OF MUSSOLINI

When Mussolini was fired, the Italian government held him captive in a resort hotel in the Gran Sasso mountains in central Italy. Adolf Hitler sent special forces led by Otto Skorzeny to get him. The rescuers landed next to the hotel in gliders and found Mussolini. He and Skorzeny then flew to Vienna, Austria.

casualties. It took four attempts before the Allies reached the summit of Monte Cassino on May 18. In all, some 45,000 Axis and Allied troops had been killed or wounded.

Landings at Anzio

Meanwhile, the Allies began Operation Shingle, an amphibious landing north of the Gustav Line. Major-General John Lucas landed the U.S. VI Corps at Anzio on January 22, 1944. The Germans were unprepared and the landings were a

➔ Large U.S. landing craft loom over the harbor at Anzio after the Allied landings in January 1944.

the hill town of Cassino. The early arrival of a bitterly cold Italian winter hampered their operation.

Dominated by a 16th-century Benedictine monastery, Cassino was defended by battle-hardened German panzer troops and elite paratroopers. The battle for the town was one of the bloodiest of the whole European war. The first Allied offensive on the Gustav Line began on January 17, 1944, and suffered heavy

← U.S. troops drive past the ancient Colosseum during the liberation of Rome on June 5, 1944.

success, but Lucas's delay in moving his troops turned the operation into a disaster. The Germans attacked the Allies, causing 5,100 casualties in just six days.

The Tide Turns

By mid-February, the German advance threatened to push the Allies back into the sea. After a long siege, VI Corps finally joined up with II Corps on May 25.

U.S. troops broke through the Gustav Line and entered Rome on June 5, 1944. Fighting continued in Italy until the Germans surrendered on April 29, 1945. The battle for Italy had cost 312,000 Allied and 434,000 German casualties.

THE EASTERN FRONT

Despite signing a nonaggression pact with the Soviet leader, Joseph Stalin, in summer 1940 Hitler ordered his commanders to plan the invasion of the Soviet Union.

The German plan, Operation Barbarossa, was based on speed. Hitler and his generals planned to defeat the Red Army in five weeks. The timetable was strict; any delay would leave the army fighting in a Russian winter for which it was not prepared.

The Germans gathered one of the largest invasion forces ever seen: more than 3 million soldiers, 3,580 tanks, more than 7,000 artillery guns and almost 2,000 aircraft. There would be three massive thrusts: Army Group North would advance to Leningrad; Army Group South would advance to the Ukrainian capital, Kiev; and Army Group

← Soviet infantry wait to board a train to the front. Stalin had a seemingly endless supply of men.

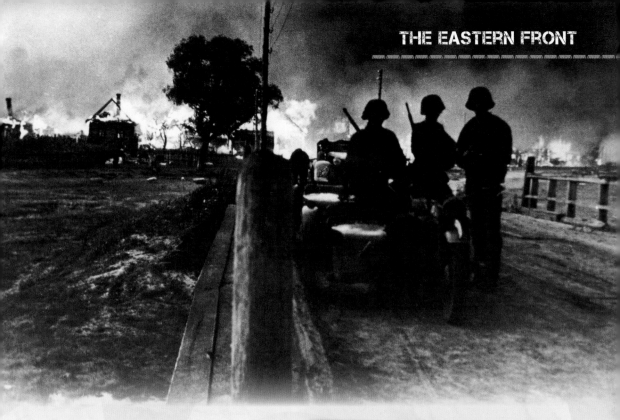

⬆ German soldiers watch a village burn as they advance. The western Soviet Union was devastated in the invasion.

Center would advance to Moscow. Despite warning signs, Stalin and his generals were caught unprepared. The Red Army lacked the organization and equipment of the German invasion force. On June 22, 1941—later than planned due to Hitler's negotiations in southeastern Europe—German troops invaded Soviet territory. In the first few weeks of the invasion, their advance appeared unstoppable. By the end of July, Army Group North was three-quarters of the way to Leningrad.

The German invasion was not going entirely to plan, however. The German

THE BALKANS AND GREECE

Before Hitler launched Operation Barbarossa, he turned to southeastern Europe, where Romania had valuable oil fields. Hitler persuaded Hungary, Romania, and Bulgaria to join the Axis. Yugoslavia and Greece resisted, but were both conquered in April 1941. The fighting delayed Barbarossa by five weeks—a delay that would prove disastrous when the Soviet winter came.

KEY EVENTS

← German soldiers fight alongside a Panzer Mark III as they advance into a Soviet town.

planners had misjudged the problem of supplying the troops on poor roads. The farther east the Germans moved, the more difficult it was to provide them with food, fuel, and spare parts.

Fall of Kiev

Stalin had ordered Kiev to be defended at all costs, but the city fell on September 19, 1941. The Wehrmacht murdered many of the inhabitants, including 34,000 Jews. Hitler saw Kiev as a magnificent victory but many of his commanders thought it was a strategic error that diverted troops south from the key advance on Moscow.

KEY PEOPLE

JOSEPH STALIN

Joseph Stalin rose through the ranks of the Communist Party and seized the Soviet leadership in 1924. In the late 1920s his farm reforms resulted in famines that starved millions of citizens. In the mid-1930s Stalin began killing his political opponents by the thousands, including senior military officers. Despite warnings, Stalin refused to believe the Germans would attack in June 1941. This refusal led to disaster for the Red Army. Later, however, Stalin listened to the advice of his generals— unlike Adolf Hitler.

Meanwhile citizens in Leningrad built barricades and ditches around the city. By the end of August, German troops were on the outskirts. A siege began that lasted 900 days.

Operation Typhoon

The diversion of troops south to Kiev weakened Army Group Center, which was just 200 miles (325 km) from Moscow. A final advance—Operation Typhoon—began on October 3 but was halted when rains turned the roads to mud. When the cold weather froze the roads in early November, the advance resumed. By November 27, the Germans were just 20 miles (32 km) from Moscow.

The Soviets had two advantages, however. First, reinforcements arrived from Siberia, so Marshal Georgy Zhukov, chief-in-staff of the Red Army, had some 720,000 troops, 1,700 tanks, 8,000 guns and 1,400 aircraft around Moscow by the beginning of December. Second, the winter turned out to be the coldest for 50 years. The Germans were unprepared for such bitter conditions, and many froze to death. Vehicles and weapons also froze. It was clear that the Germans could not win. On December 4, Hitler agreed to a retreat from Moscow.

⬇ Wearing special winter clothing, Soviet infantry counterattack near Moscow.

➔ This Russian naval cabin boy won a medal for fighting in the Battle of Sevastopol in the Crimea.

Soviet Counterattack

Armed with a new weapon—the Katyusha rocket launcher—the Soviets smashed into the German retreat, which became chaotic. Hitler ordered the retreat to stop and by the end of December a German line had been set up. By mid-February the Soviet counteroffensive had lost much of its momentum. By March 1942, casualties on both sides

KEY EVENTS

SNIPERS IN STALINGRAD

The ruins of Stalingrad were ideal for snipers. Snipers lay in wait to shoot the enemy from long range. Both sides trained snipers, and Soviet snipers included several women. The snipers were expert at blending into their surroundings and lying still for hours. They killed many enemy officers and soldiers and created fear in their opponents.

were so high as to be unsustainable: German casualties stood at 1,150,00 and Soviet casualties were at least 4 million. Hitler, however, planned another major offensive. He sent part of Army Group South into the Caucasus, on the border between Europe and Asia, to seize oil fields there. The rest of the army group—the Sixth Army and parts of the Fourth Panzer Army—headed for Stalingrad.

Stalingrad

The Battle of Stalingrad, fought between August 23, 1942, and February 2, 1943, marked a turning point in the European war. Stalingrad was an industrial city on the River Volga in the southwest Soviet

Union. As the Germans advanced, Stalin ordered the citizens to dig antitank ditches, bunkers, and embankments around oil storage tanks.

Germans Attack

On August 23, the Luftwaffe started to bomb Stalingrad. On September 13, German troops advanced into the shattered city, where they met stubborn resistance. As fighting raged, dust created by the bombardment made it difficult to tell soldiers apart. Many were killed by their own side. Soviet civilians hid in cellars and sewers with virtually no food. By November 12, the German attack had slowed down with Soviet troops still holding small pockets of the city. Snipers fired from the ruins while men fought hand-to-hand in the devastated streets in what the Germans called the *Rattenkrieg* (War of the Rats).

Operation Uranus

General Georgy K. Zhukov, Stalin's second-in-command, launched a counteroffensive on November 19. He had assembled more than one million men, 1,000 tanks and 14,000 heavy guns. By November 22, the Soviet forces had encircled the Sixth Army. Hitler ordered his own counteroffensive, Operation Winter Storm, to relieve the

⬇ German infantry take cover in a trench during the fighting in the ruins of Stalingrad.

THE T-34 TANK

In 1941 German Field Marshal Ewald von Kleist called the Soviet T-34 "the finest tank in the world." The Soviets produced almost 40,000 T-34s during the war. The tank was faster, more maneuverable, and better armored than its German equivalents. Its hull was angled so that enemy shells bounced off it, while its 76mm gun could pierce any enemy tank.

To prove to the world and Stalin that Germany was still a force to be reckoned with, Hitler sent one of his most able commanders, Field Marshal Erich von Manstein, to stabilize the front.

Manstein recaptured Kharkov before rains halted his counterattack. He gathered forces for another thrust, named Operation Citadel. By the summer of 1943, two-thirds of the German Army was on the Soviet front ready to attack the Soviet line at Kursk. In fact, it was the Soviets who attacked first, on July 5, 1943. By July 10, the Germans had suffered serious losses. The biggest tank battle of the war took place on July 12 at

siege, but the Luftwaffe could not keep the Sixth Army supplied by airdrops. By December, the Germans were eating rats. By February 1943, they had run out of ammunition. The Sixth Army surrendered.

Battle of Kursk

After the defeat at Stalingrad, the Germans retreated in the face of a Soviet counteroffensive that recaptured the key city of Kharkov in Ukraine, which had been in German hands since late 1941.

→ German tanks and armored vehicles wait to go into action in the Battle of Kursk.

→ German soldiers round up Soviet partisans— guerrilla fighters—from their hideout in a barn.

Prokhorovka, 50 miles (80 km) southeast of Kursk. By nightfall, the Germans had lost another 10,000 men and another 350 tanks.

By July 23, the Germans had been pushed back to their starting point. They suffered 200,000 casualties at Kursk, the Soviets 800,000. The Germans lost 1,500 tanks to the Soviets' 1,800. But although neither side won a clear victory, the losses the Germans had sustained at Kharkov and Kursk meant they were no longer the threat they had once been. From now on they would be on the defensive on the Eastern Front.

THE INVASION OF EUROPE

Allied commanders knew the only way to defeat Hitler was to invade northern Europe. Stalin was also eager for an attack to relieve pressure on the Eastern Front.

In January 1943, the Allies began to plan an attack across the English Channel to Normandy in northern France. It would take time to assemble the troops and equipment needed for what was named Operation Overlord. The attack was planned for June 1944.

For their part, the Germans knew the Allied attack would come at some point. Hitler was convinced the location would be at Pas de Calais in eastern France. Field Marshal Erwin Rommel, who was in charge of the Channel defenses, believed an attack would come further west. He strengthened the so-called Atlantic Wall with obstacles and gun positions to stop any advance from the beaches.

→ British soldiers practice crossing barbed wire in preparation for D-Day.

↑ The Allied High Command for D-Day, including General Eisenhower (front, center).

Landings in France

With U.S. and British troops trained in secret, D-Day (the day on which Operation Overlord was due to begin) was scheduled for June 5, 1944. Bad weather delayed it by 24 hours. Just before midnight on June 6, about 23,500 Allied paratroopers and glider troops landed near the five landing beaches in Normandy to seize bridges and communications centers.

On June 6, U.S. troops successfully landed at Utah Beach. By 9:00 a.m., the first tanks had crossed the Atlantic

THE RESISTANCE

To support Operation Overlord, the Allies called on the help of about 100,000 members of the French Resistance. British and U.S. agents had been to France to arm the Resistance, carry out sabotage, and gather information. Their main target was the rail system, which the Germans would use to move troops to meet the landings. The Resistance carried out raids on railroads before and during D-Day.

KEY THEMES

DWIGHT D. EISENHOWER

Some people thought U.S. general Eisenhower was an odd choice to lead a huge assault. He had relatively little combat experience. But Eisenhower had led the U.S. capture of Tunisia in May 1943 and was expert at developing strategy. His decision to advance on a broad front in northwest Europe in 1944 proved largely successful.

⬇ British troops unload a jeep and other equipment from a glider on D-Day.

Wall to move inland. By nightfall, 23,000 men and 1,700 vehicles had made it ashore at Utah Beach. On Omaha Beach, 10 miles (16 km) to the east, it was another story. Many landing craft stopped too far from the beach, and hundreds of soldiers drowned. Those who made it ashore came under heavy fire from German defenders. Although 30,000 men made it ashore by dusk another, 2,300 had been killed in what was almost a disaster. British and Canadian forces had more success on Gold, Sword, and Juno beaches.

Battle of Normandy

By the end of D-Day, 128,000 Allied soldiers were ashore. Behind them hundreds of thousands more troops were setting out from England. Their task was to take the towns of Caen and Bayeux to

⬆ Allied vehicles line the shore as U.S. troops land on Omaha Beach late on D-Day.

help the Allies break out of Normandy. Moving through the Normandy countryside was difficult because of the *bocage*. This landscape of small fields and narrow lanes separated by tall hedge-covered banks made it difficult for Allied tanks to advance, but it was ideal country for German troops to ambush Allied infantry. Poor weather delayed the arrival of supplies from England, which further slowed down the Allied assault. By the end of June, Allied casualties stood at 62,000 and they had advanced just a few miles inland from the landing beaches.

EYEWITNESS ACCOUNT

"Back and forth the bomb carpets were laid, artillery positions were wiped out, tanks overturned and buried, infantry positions flattened, and roads and tracks destroyed. By midday, the entire area resembled a moon landscape, with the bomb craters touching rim to rim. The shock effect on the men was indescribable."

Fritz Bayerlein
Panzer Lehr Division,
Normandy, August 1944

GEORGE S. PATTON

Patton was a controversial U.S. officer who made his name during the landings in North Africa in 1942. He was sidelined after slapping sick soldiers but returned to duty in July 1944. He led the U.S. Third Army in a series of fast-moving offensives. He reacted quickly to block the German advance in the Ardennes and his troops were among the first across the Rhine River.

The Allies changed tactics, sending the U.S. Third Army of General George S. Patton into Brittany to capture St. Lô to try to find an alternative route out of Normandy. Patton was an expert in fast-moving armored warfare, and his army moved through Brittany meeting little resistance.

The Falaise Pocket

The Anglo-Canadian force at Caen began to drive south on August 7. Meanwhile, the U.S. forces drove north. The two met at Falaise on August 19. They surrounded 100,000 Germans in an area measuring just 20 by 10 miles

Allied Breakout

The town of Caen, with its vital rail and road links, remained in German hands despite repeated Allied attacks. On July 7, the Allies made another attempt on the town when they launched Operation Charnwood. After two days of fighting, Anglo-Canadian forces were finally able to capture Caen. As the Germans withdrew, however, they blew up all bridges over the Orne River. The Allies were still stranded and unable to break out to the east.

➜ In the days after D-Day, supplies pour ashore for the Allies.

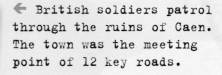

← British soldiers patrol through the ruins of Caen. The town was the meeting point of 12 key roads.

(32 by 16 km). Defying Hitler's orders to fight to the death, some 40,000 German troops escaped from Caen and retreated. It was a great Allied victory: 10,000 German soldiers were killed and 50,000 captured.

The Allies had broken out of Normandy and poured toward the western border of Nazi Germany. Meanwhile, in southern France, another Allied landing had taken place on August 15. The 175,000 Allied troops of Operation Anvil met little resistance as they pushed the Germans out of southern France. On September 11, they linked up with Patton's Third Army outside the city of Dijon.

On August 19, as the Allied forces approached Paris, the capital's citizens rose up against the German garrison. Hitler ordered that the city be destroyed, but the local German commander disobeyed his orders. Five days later, Free French troops led the Allies into the capital amid great celebrations.

By early September 1944, the Allied drive east to the German border was slowing because of a lack of supplies landing in

Normandy. A port closer to the troops was needed for resupplying. One possible target was Antwerp in Belgium, which was captured by British and Canadian troops on October 8 after weeks of fighting.

Meanwhile the Allies launched Operation Market Garden, a thrust through the Netherlands into northern Germany. The attack aimed to encircle the important industrial area of the Ruhr. However, the armored advance did not advance quickly enough before the Germans destroyed key bridges over the Rhine River. The failure of Operation Market Garden meant that the war in Europe would last for another eight months.

The Battle of the Bulge

During the winter of 1944–1945, Hitler made one last attempt to split the advancing Allies in two and prevent them landing supplies via Antwerp. On December 16 the Germans attacked a weak part of the Allied line in the hilly, thickly wooded Ardennes Forest in Belgium and Luxembourg.

← British troops take cover in Arnhem, Holland, during Operation Market Garden.

⬆ U.S. ammunition carriers make their way through a snowy wood during the Battle of the Bulge.

The Germans made early gains, creating a bulge in the Allied lines that gave the battle its name. Although they were outnumbered, U.S. forces held firm at the sides of the bulge, particularly at Bastogne. Unable to expand their attack, the Germans knew the assault had failed.

Hitler had gambled everything on the attack in the Ardennes. Some 120,000 men were killed or injured, and Hitler had run out of reserves. The fighting had delayed the Allies' final offensive against Germany by just six weeks.

JULY BOMB PLOT

By 1944 some Germans believed Hitler was the main obstacle to making peace with the Allies. Some of his advisors plotted to murder him. On July 20, 1944, Count Claus Schenk von Stauffenberg took a briefcase into a meeting with Hitler. He then left the room. A bomb inside the briefcase blew up, causing considerable damage. Hitler escaped with minor injuries. The plotters were rounded up and killed.

KEY EVENTS

THE FALL OF GERMANY

By February 1945, the Allies were in a position to begin the conquest of Germany. U.S. and British troops advanced from the west and the Soviet Red Army from the east.

In the west, Allied commanders raced to be first across the Rhine River and into Germany. British troops under Field Marshal Bernard Montgomery reached the river on February 8, 1945, and began bombarding German positions. As the Germans fell back across the river, they blew up most of the bridges. However, the Allies captured one bridge at Remagen, south of Cologne. It was a vital crossing point for the Allies.

Despite being farthest from the Rhine, General George S. Patton's Third Army were the first Allies to cross the river. Montgomery had been reinforcing his troops ready to cross the Rhine on March 23, 1945, but Patton crossed by boat the night before. With further crossings on March 23, the Allies established three bridgeheads on the eastern bank of the

↑ Men of the U.S. Third Army keep their heads low to avoid snipers as they cross the Rhine River in March 1945.

⬆ Soviet tanks enter Berlin after the Allies agreed they would capture the city.

Rhine. They faced three German army groups but the Germans were using poorly trained reservists, military typists, and cooks to bolster the fighting units.

In Berlin, Hitler was losing his grip on reality. Still believing in ultimate German victory, he ordered his units to keep fighting. He had made Field Marshal Albert Kesselring his new commander-in-chief, but Kesselring did not have the forces to halt the Allied advance.

The next Allied objective was the Elbe River, which was just 45 miles (70 km) west of Berlin. From there, the Allied

YALTA CONFERENCE

In February 1945 the three Allied leaders—Roosevelt, Churchill, and Stalin—met at Yalta in the Crimea, in the Soviet Union, to discuss the final defeat of Hitler. They decided to divide Germany into zones of occupation. They also agreed that the Soviets would be left in control of much of eastern Europe. The Soviets promised to allow free elections, but in reality eastern Europe would be governed by communist puppet regimes.

KEY EVENTS

DRESDEN RAID

On the night of February 13-14, 1945, 800 Allied bombers dropped 3,000 tons of bombs on the historic German city of Dresden. The bombs started fires that combined to form a firestorm. Estimates of the death toll in Dresden range from 40,000 to 100,000. So many civilians died that people protested even in the Allied nations. Many people began to question the morality of so-called carpet bombing.

commanders expected to launch a final assault on Berlin, but this was no longer possible. In February 1945, the Allied leaders had met at Yalta, in Crimea on the Black Sea, and agreed that the Soviet Red Army would lead the assault on Berlin from the east. On April 25, 1945, U.S. and Soviet forces met for the first time near Torgau on the Elbe. The two Allied advances had come together.

The Soviet Offensive

Since the Battle of Kursk in July 1943, Soviet forces had been on the offensive. Through the fall they liberated much of Ukraine, before halting to build up an overwhelming advantage in men and equipment for another attack.

➜ Tanks and trucks of the U.S. Third Army cross a river in Austria in May 1945.

Operation Bagration, in summer 1944, destroyed Germany's Army Group Center and liberated Belorussia. German resistance was disappearing.

The western Allies had suffered huge casualties in their campaign, but the losses on the Eastern Front were far greater. The Soviet advances from late 1944 until the fall of Berlin in May 1945 cost the Soviets more dead than the British and United States suffered in the entire war in all theaters.

↑ **The last photograph of Hitler before his death shows him awarding medals to members of the Hitler Youth.**

The Red Army in Germany

The four Red Army fronts (groups) that struck into Germany consisted of nearly four million men, 10,000 aircraft, 3,300 tanks, and 28,000 artillery pieces. The advance was led by the Soviets' two most able commanders, Marshal Georgy Zhukov, who led the 1st Belorussian Front, and Marshal Ivan Konev, who led the 1st Ukrainian Front. Facing them were around 600,000 German soldiers commanded by Heinrich Himmler, head of the Schutzstaffel (SS, the security police). Hitler had put Himmler in charge as a reward for his loyalty, rather than because of his military skill.

The Soviets Arrive

The Soviet advance on Germany, the Vistula–Oder Offensive, was the largest single offensive of World War II. It started on January 12, 1945. German resistance soon melted away. In East Prussia, which was the first German territory the Soviets entered, many thousands of panicking East Prussian civilians tried to escape by ship from one of the Baltic ports.

Further south, the Red Army advanced through Poland, capturing the capital, Warsaw, on January 17, 1945. By the end of the Vistula–Oder Offensive on February 3, the Red Army had advanced

355 miles (570 km), liberating the whole of Poland and most of Czechoslovakia, and isolating two German panzer armies in East Prussia. Soviet troops were now on the Oder River, only 37.5 miles (60 km) from Berlin itself.

On February 13, the Hungarian capital, Budapest, fell to the Soviets. The campaign to retake Vienna, the capital of Austria, started on March 16. Austria's mountainous terrain made the advance difficult and the Soviets did not

⬇ A Soviet soldier is depicted raising the Red Flag of the Soviet Union above Berlin on May 2, 1945.

reach the city until April 5. In eight days of fighting, much of the historic center was destroyed. The city fell on April 13.

The Battle of Berlin

Inside Berlin, Hitler had ordered every male to defend the city. Anyone found not fighting risked being hanged from lamposts by SS men who roamed the streets. The city was defended by about one million men, but many were elderly or were young boys, and few were properly trained. Hitler retreated to his bunker, which lay deep beneath the Chancellery. From there, he ordered the defense of the city to continue, although there were 2.5 million Soviet soldiers waiting to attack.

The Soviets started to bomb the city on April 16, 1945. By April 25, they had the city surrounded. The Red Army made its way through the city street by street. Soviet bombers reduced the city to rubble. German resistance remained strong, but by April 27, the Germans only held 15 square miles (38 sqkm) of the city. On April 30, with Soviet troops just half a mile away, Hitler committed suicide in his bunker.

The Nazi leadership passed to the commander of the Navy, Grand Admiral Karl Dönitz. The German High Command rejected Soviet demands for surrender, but on May 2, 1945, the commandant of Berlin surrendered the city. The fight for the city had cost about 300,000 German and Soviet dead. Five days later, Germany signed its total surrender. The war in Europe was over.

↑ New Yorkers celebrate Victory in Europe (VE) Day on May 8, 1945. Fighting in Japan continued for three more months.

THE DEATH OF HITLER

From April 20 to April 30, 1945, Adolf Hitler lived in the bunker beneath the Chancellery. With him were his mistress, Eva Braun, high-ranking Nazi officials, and domestic staff. By then, Hitler was physically and mentally sick. He burst out in furious rages. Even his closest allies began to desert him. They wanted to make peace. On April 29, Hitler learned that Soviet forces were only a block away. He married Eva Braun. The next day they committed suicide. Braun took poison, while Hitler shot himself. Their bodies were burned.

KEY PEOPLE

TIMELINE OF WORLD WAR II

1939   **September:** German troops invade and overrun Poland; Britain and France declare war on Germany; the Soviet Union invades eastern Poland. The Battle of the Atlantic begins.

April: Germany invades Denmark and Norway; Allied troops land in Norway.

May: Germany invades Luxembourg, the Netherlands, Belgium, and France; Allied troops are evacuated at Dunkirk.

June: Allied troops leave Norway; Italy enters the war; France signs an armistice with Germany; Italy bombs Malta in the Mediterranean.

July: German submarines (U-boats) inflict heavy losses on Allied convoys in the Atlantic; The Battle of Britain begins.

September: Luftwaffe air raids begin the Blitz—the bombing of British cities; Italian troops advance from Libya into Egypt.

October: Italy invades Greece.

December: British troops defeat the Italians at Sidi Barrani, Egypt.

1941   **January:** Allied units capture Tobruk in Libya.

February: Rommel's Afrika Korps arrive in Tripoli.

March: The Afrika Korps drive British troops back from El Agheila.

April: Axis units invade Yugoslavia; German forces invade Greece; the Afrika Korps besiege Tobruk.

June: German troops invade the Soviet Union.

September: Germans besiege Leningrad and attack Moscow.

December: Japanese aircraft attack the U.S. Pacific Fleet at Pearl Harbor; Japanese forces invade the Philippines, Malaya, and Thailand, and defeat the British garrison in Hong Kong.

1942   **January:** Japan invades Burma; Rommel launches a new offensive in Libya; Allied troops leave Malaya.

February: Singapore surrenders to the Japanese.

April: The Bataan Peninsula in the Philippines falls to the Japanese.

May: U.S. and Japanese fleets clash at the Battle of the Coral Sea.

June: The U.S. Navy defeats the Japanese at the Battle of Midway; Rommel recaptures Tobruk.

September–October: Allied forces defeat Axis troops at El Alamein, Egypt, the first major Allied victory of the war.

November: U.S. and British troops land in Morocco and Algeria.

1943

February: The German Sixth Army surrenders at Stalingrad; the Japanese leave Guadalcanal in the Solomon Islands.

May: Axis forces in Tunisia surrender.

July: The Red Army wins the Battle of Kursk; Allied troops land on the Italian island of Sicily.

August: German forces occupy Italy; the Soviets retake Kharkov.

September: Allied units begin landings on mainland Italy; Italy surrenders, prompting a German invasion of northern Italy.

November: U.S. carrier aircraft attack Rabaul in the Solomon Islands.

1944

January: The German siege of Leningrad ends.

February: U.S. forces conquer the Marshall Islands.

March: The Soviet offensive reaches the Dniester River; Allied aircraft bomb the monastery at Monte Cassino in Italy.

June: U.S. troops enter the city of Rome; D-Day–the Allied invasion of northern Europe; U.S. aircraft defeat the Japanese fleet at the Battle of the Philippine Sea.

July: Soviet tanks enter Poland.

August: Japanese troops retreat in Burma; Allied units liberate towns in France, Belgium, and the Netherlands.

October: The Japanese suffer defeat at the Battle of Leyte Gulf.

December: German troops counterattack in the Ardennes.

1945

January: The U.S. Army lands on Luzon in the Philippines; most of Poland and Czechoslovakia are liberated by the Allies.

February: U.S. troops land on Iwo Jima; Soviet troops strike west across Germany; the U.S. Army heads toward the Rhine River.

April: U.S. troops land on the island of Okinawa; Mussolini is shot by partisans; Soviet troops assault Berlin; Hitler commits suicide.

May: All active German forces surrender.

June: Japanese resistance ends in Burma and on Okinawa.

August: Atomic bombs are dropped on Hiroshima and Nagasaki; Japan surrenders.

GLOSSARY

advance A general move forward by a military force.

Allies One of the two groups of combatants in the war. The main Allies were Britain, the Soviet Union, the United States, British Empire troops, and free forces from occupied nations.

amphibious landing A landing from the sea, usually by infantry and artillery supported by naval and air power.

armistice An agreement made by two sides in a war to stop fighting in order to hold peace talks.

armor A term referring to armored vehicles, such as tanks.

artillery Large weapons such as big guns and howitzers.

Axis One of two groups of combatans in the war. The main Axis powers were Germany, Italy, and Japan.

counteroffensive A set of attacks launched as a defense against enemy attacks.

dogfight A close combat between fighter aircraft.

fascist Someone who believes in a dictatorial, militaristic political system.

flank The right or left side of a military advance.

garrison A group of soldiers placed to defend a specific location.

guerrilla A member of a small group who attacks larger forces using irregular tactics such as ambush and sabotage.

hoax A deliberate attempt to deceive someone.

infantry Soldiers who are trained to fight on foot, or in vehicles.

landing craft Shallow-bottomed boats designed to carry soldiers and supplies from ships to the shore.

Luftwaffe The German Air Force.

Marine A soldier who serves in close association with naval forces.

offensive A planned military attack.

panzer A German word for a tank.

partisans Members of armed groups fighting German occupation in Italy, Yugoslavia, or eastern Europe.

puppet government A government that appears to govern, but which is controlled by another government.

reconnaissance A small-scale survey of enemy territory to gather information.

regime A nondemocratic government.

sabotage To deliberately destroy something for military advantage.

strategy A detailed plan for achieving success.

Wehrmacht The German Army.

FURTHER RESOURCES

Books

George, Enzo. *World War II in Europe and North Africa: Preserving Democracy*. Voices of War. New York: Cavendish Square Publishing, 2014.

Hamilton, John. *Early Battles*. World War II. Edina, MN: Abdo, 2011.

Havers, Robin. *World War II: The Europe 1939–1943*. World War II: Essential Histories. New York: Rosen Publishing Group, 2010.

Jeffrey, Gary, and Terry Riley. *The Western Front*. Graphic Modern History: World War II. New York: Crabtree Publishing Company, 2012.

Samuels, Charlie. *World War II Day by Day: Europe and North Africa*. Brown Bear Books, 2013.

Websites

www.ducksters.com/history/world_war_ii/
Ducksters.com links to articles about the war.

www.pbs.org/thewar/
PBS pages on the war to support the Ken Burns' film, *The War.*

www.historyplace.com/worldwar2/timeline/ww2time.htm
Timeline of the war in Europe from Historyplace.com.

www.pbs.org/wgbh/amex/dday/
PBS pages to support the *American Experience* documentary *D-Day*

www.historynet.com/world-war-ii-north-africa-campaign.htm
Historynet pages on the campaign in North Africa.

INDEX

Afrika Korps 11–15
Anzio 20, 21
Ardennes 36, 37
armistice, Italian 18, 19
Austria 40, 42

Balkans 23
Bastogne 37
Battle of Britain 6–7
Berlin 39, 40
Berlin, Battle of 42–43
Blitz 7, 8–9
bombing 7, 8–9, 40
Bulge, Battle of the 36–37

Caen 34–35
Caucasus 26
Churchill, Winston 5, 12
Crete 11

D-Day 31-32
Dresden Raid 40

East Africa 10, 11
East Prussia 41, 42
Eastern Front 22–29, 41
Egypt 10, 11
Eisenhower, General Dwight
    D. 16, 31, 32
El Alamein 12–14

Gazala Line 12
Great Britain 6–9
Greece 11, 23
Gustav Line 19, 20, 21

Himmler, Heinrich 41
Hitler, Adolf 6, 8, 14, 17, 26,
    30, 37, 39, 41, 42, 43
Hungary 42

Italy 10, 16–21

July Bomb Plot 37

Kesselring, Field Marshal
    Albert 18, 19, 39
Kharkov 28
Kursk 28–29, 40

Leningrad 22, 23, 25
Libya 10, 12
London 7, 8, 9
Luftwaffe 6, 7, 8, 9, 27

Mediterranean Sea 11, 15
Monte Cassino 18, 19, 20
Montgomery, Bernard 13,
    16, 18, 38
Moscow 23, 24, 25
Mussolini, Benito 10, 18, 20

Normandy, Battle of 32–35
North Africa 4, 9, 10–15

Omaha Beach 32, 33
Operation Barbarossa 22–23
Operation Market Garden
    36
Operation Mincemeat 16–17
Operation Overlord 30–32
Operation Sealion 4, 8, 9
Operation Torch 14

Paris, liberation of 35
Patton, General George S.
    18, 34, 38
Poland 41, 42

Red Army 40, 43
Resistance, French 31
Rhine River 36, 38
Rome 19, 21
Rommel, Major General
    Erwin 11–15, 30
Royal Air Force 6, 9

Sicily 16–18
Skorzeny, Otto 20
snipers 26, 27
Soviet Union 9, 22–23, 39
Stalin, Joseph 24
Stalingrad 23, 26–28
Stauffenberg, Count Claus
    von 37
surrender, German 43

T-34 tank 28
Tunisia 14, 15, 32

Utah Beach 31–32

Victory in Europe Day 43
Vistula–Oder Offensive 41

Yalta Conference 39, 40
Yugoslavia 23

Zhukov, Marshal Georgy 25,
    27, 41